MW01681170

Awakening of the Spirit

by Abram Brummett

Awakening of the Spirit

ABRAM BRUMMETT

A true story about the experiences of one family and a house...

Awakening of the Spirit is an original non-fiction manuscript written by Abram Brummett and copy written in Fall of 2002.

ISBN 1-58961-369-4

Published by PageFree Publishing, Inc.
109 South Farmer Street
Otsego, Michigan 49078
1-269-692-3926
www.pagefreepublishing.com

A special thanks goes to his grandfather Leonard Brummett for the contribution of his talent towards all the sketch art in the book. I also owe much appreciation to my good friend Penny Smith whose consistently brutal honesty and drive for perfection in everything she touches has raised the quality of this book to a level I could have never hoped to attain on my own.

For Mom and Dad

For always believing me when I spoke the truth, no matter how crazy it sounded, and for always supporting me in whatever I wanted to do, teaching me there are no limits in life.

"Life is eternal; and love is immortal; and death is only a horizon; and a horizon is nothing save the limit of our sight."

- *R. W. Raymond*

Chapters

Can you see yourself rummaging through your closet looking for that pair of shoes that you haven't been able to find in ages? You know they're in there somewhere but it will take a little determination and some luck if you're going to find them. You dive in literally head first and start pushing stuff around. Out of the corner of your eye in the back of the closet you see the shoes you're looking for. You reach back to grab them and as you pick them up you notice they were sitting on something that catches your eye. A small book is lying there on the floor of your closet. You've never seen it before and as you're about to leave your closet with the shoes your curiosity gets the best of you. You pick up the book and your eyes focus on the title as you blow the dust off the cover. Flipping open to the first few pages you start reading and realize it's a ghost story, a first hand account of one family and a house they lived in for several years. You read a few pages of this documentary that serves as a window into the experiences this family underwent. Interest peaks, so you read on, going deeper into the story with the family and reliving their poltergeist experience that has been held timeless on the pages within. You remember skimming by a page in the front of the book that had a sketch on it. You flip back to that page with the sketch and see a picture of your house, the house that you live in. The book that you now hold in your hands will someday be that very book that the next owner of this house on Kansas Street will pull out of that deep closet in the second story room where I grew up. We all have ways of conveying the stories of our lives that have had integral roles in shaping us to be the people we are today, and this is mine.

Introduction

Haunted houses have always attracted attention. The picture that comes to mind is one of a tall old house on a hill usually hiding some kind of creaky staircase inside the front door. In the movies we usually see a house that has its shutters dangling by a rusty nail and the generally large structure of the home itself resembling a sinisterly twisted face ready to devour you upon entrance. There is almost certainly a long gravel driveway that requires traversing down an ominous path with a rickety iron gate to the heavy lion headed knocker that tries to warn you one last time to run for your life before it's too late.

But my house looks like just another house on the block. You won't find a terrifying front door that seems to eat people as they come in or gravestones near gangly dead trees in the front yard. It is just a regular house with two stories, well secured red shutters, and a front porch perfectly suited for spending afternoons reading or napping as your mood suggests.

My name is Abram and I have a story to tell. What my family and I have gone through in this house is not the trite bump in the night stuff you watch on the Discovery Channel or hear over a camp fire. You don't often hear of a ghost changing someone's life but I can assuredly say that the things I encountered in my house have forever changed me. What happened to my family in our quaint hundred year old home was as mysteriously confusing as it was real. Even today I can't really be sure what we encountered but it's the fact that we encountered something unlike anything I had ever confronted before that has left a lasting impact on my life.

Until this past year I had always respected the spirits in my home but never really had any major experiences with them. The occasional electrical appliance coming on at random or hearing bumps in the night were scary nonetheless, but not the hundred percent proof I needed to truly believe without a doubt that my house was indeed haunted or that there was even any sort of life after death. In fact, if you would have asked me what I believed in before the experiences that follow on these pages, I would have told you that I didn't believe in anything at all.

As far as religion went, it was something that I had all but given up on. I figured since nobody could have known enough to have an idea of what they were talking about then there was no point in trying to figure anything out. I knew that if I were going to believe in God or follow a particular faith, I would need to have good reasons. I've never really been the hop-in-the-current-and-kick-back type. Human herding has always kind of rubbed me the wrong way.

After the events of the last year there have been remarkable changes in myself and my family. I have begun living a very spiritual lifestyle and am actively searching out God's will in my life. Myself, and my two younger siblings, Hannah and Eli, have been baptized; if you told me a year ago that this was going to happen I would have never believed it. Thinking back on everything that has happened to my family over the past nine years, it really is remarkable to realize how priceless of an experience it all has been. Although at times some of us really had to suffer through some mild hysterical psychosis, I believe now that it's all said and done; the end has justified the means. I have my personal proof of the afterlife. I have found my proof of God. A *knowing* of these things is something that I value very highly and am very thankful for. It just blows my mind when I think about all the people out there who haven't experienced what I have and in turn still question things like, "Do we live on after we die?" I just wish I could convey all of my experiences to someone by simply sharing the memory with them. That way they could actually see everything as I did, which has brought me to the mindset and knowledge I have today. But since this is not possible I am doing the next best thing by putting it all down in writing for people to hopefully learn something from. All the events in this book are absolutely true, absolutely real, and all I can do is ask you to take my word for it.

Chapter One

This house just feels right...

In the spring of 1994, my family traveled from Columbia, Missouri to Edwardsville, Illinois with our two dogs and several vehicles stuffed to the brim with our every belonging. Our grandparents waited with my brother, Eli, sister, Hannah, myself and our two dogs while my parents went to sign the papers for the house. We anxiously waited around for them to return with the keys so we could enter our new house on Kansas Street for the first time as the rightful owners.

Finally they showed up and we immediately set to work getting our stuff unpacked and into the home. The two big dogs, Yeti, a Great Pyrenees, and Dusty, a golden retriever, were going crazy running from room to room claiming their territory and inspecting every inch of the new home. A few seconds after we had stepped into the house my Dad said, "Oh yeah, while we were signing the papers for the house the seller, Betty Davis, put down her pen and said she should probably tell us about Emily."

"Who?" I asked, stopping in my tracks immediately interested.

My Dad continued, "Well, she said there is a ghost in the house that used to sit upstairs in a rocking chair and play with her daughter. Her daughter just started calling her Emily and everyone in the family has had some kind of experience with the spirit."

This house had been on the market and sat empty for four years. Betty lived in Minnesota while real estate agents tried to sell her house in Edwardsville. Every now and then Betty would get phone calls from the agents letting her know that lights had come on in her empty home. Betty told us that Emily likes to play with the switches. At this point I was incredibly paranoid about the kinds of horrible plans Emily had for me and I was a little pissed off that the people around me were dismissing her behavior by saying things like, "oh she just likes to play with the switches." For me, it was time to run. But where do you go when you're thirteen years old? I just didn't think it was fair that I, being completely terrified with the concept of ghosts to begin with, had to get the house with the grandma Freddy Crougar upstairs and everybody was ok with that?! I flew through the five stages of coping with a crisis pretty fast on this one because I didn't really have any choice. Anger and denial came and went within the first few days. Then I decided I would bargain. I tried to make peace with the very thing that I thought would wake me up while attempting to drain me from the neck of my vital life force before moving on to the rest of my family. Being unsatisfied that I had reached any kind of armistice with the elusive but surely malicious inhabitant I moved on to the next stage. A brief depression of about two months gripped my young soul and was followed by the acceptance that this is where I now lived and there wasn't anything I would be able to do to change that, no matter how many ritualistic cat sacrifices I made in vain to recover some peace of mind in my day to day life.

Besides the rumored ghost, I loved the house. It had a feel about it unlike any other house I'd ever been in. Walking in, the first thing you'll probably notice is our old hardwood floors that really add character to the house, and it was character that my parents were really looking for while we shopped for a place to live. It was just as well that if a house was brand new we shouldn't even go look at it. We wanted a house with a story to tell, a house whose very walls have stood longer than our grandparents had been alive. The house that we found on Kansas Street was the only one that we all felt good about. Oddly enough when looking at the house the first time my Dad joked with the realtor that we were looking for a haunted house. Be careful what you wish for.

There is something about how a beautiful old house has so gracefully withstood Father Time that makes you respect it. I'm sure that when I get older my first house will be much like the one on Kansas Street, only perhaps without the extended inhabitants. The first floor of the home feels very calm with large openings, being too large for doors, to the rooms. It is here where we have our living room, dining room, computer room with wood burning stove, the kitchen, one bathroom, and the master bedroom. The basement of the house is very large, spanning the entire foundation, with a low ceiling that at times forces you to walk with your head tilted to the side to save on painful bumps. A cellar, photography darkroom, and bathroom inhabit this level. A particular wall in the cellar has a different look to it than the other walls in the basement. It has always made the family a little suspicious and we've always joked about knocking it down during the next family reunion. Family reunions seem to serve as good times for investigation in the home but with this particular project we never followed through.

Going up to the second floor in the home is a solid straight shot up a flight of creaky old stairs that echo as you climb them and occasionally leave you with the feeling that you are being followed. At the very top of the stairs is a short hallway that has three doorways, one to each of the three bedrooms on that floor. Being the oldest, I immediately chose the largest of the three. I was so proud of my new room, even my Dad referred to it as the football field. There was so much room I only used half of it which I covered with a cheap second hand carpet leaving the other half of the room virtually bare. A huge set of doors opened into the large closet in the corner of the room. There was a smaller, oddly shaped door next to the larger doors that opened into the same closet. This whole closet system was a recent addition to the home by the family that lived there before us. When I opened it the first time I was horrified to see over twenty spiders smashed on the floor. "That's sick" I proclaimed, but after inspecting the other rooms I figured having a few extra spiders in my closet was a small price to pay for getting the largest living space. In the ceiling of my bedroom is a small, square door with a handle used to enter the attic. Once up there, the first thing you want to do is get back down. It was your typical stuffy and oven like attic but the fact that it might have dead people was enough to make me never want to venture there again. It was the kind of place where if someone told me there was a chest full of gold in the far corner, and all I had to do was walk back and get it, I would have said no thanks. I wanted to wrap some thick chains around the handles a few times and padlock it breaking the key off inside the lock.

Anyway, back to the second floor. The room directly across from mine went to my younger brother. It would turn out that this blue room was the room that Betty's daughter lived and played in while Emily occasionally watched from her rocking chair. The room seems to watch you when you're in it. The four foot door in the corner adds creepiness to the area as you expect to see a coffin with a mummified corpse upon opening it and peering inside. Opening the small door you see a long, low, narrow closet that has the signs of time all over it. It has paint chips from the wall lying scattered onto a worn hardwood floor.

Moving back into the hallway and walking to the end there is another room that would be claimed by my sister. It's a pink room with a very low ceiling that preys on the heads of guests not used to all the ducking and dodging that is necessary to escape unscathed. This room also has a closet and a single window overlooking the street in front of the home.

So there we were, settling into our new home and leaving our old home behind. Trying to deal with the transition of picking your life up and moving it somewhere else is always a scary one. The last thing we needed to deal with at that point was a supernatural presence in our new home. My siblings and I were able to keep each other company the first summer there when we didn't know anybody else. We would spend our days in loud play upstairs mostly oblivious to any ghost that might have been trying to get our attention.

We used to play with our plastic guns and swords a lot and I can remember one day I had received a fatal wound and was lying dead in my brother's room. I could hear my brother and sister bumping around in the next room very clearly because my lifeless body had an ear pressed against the floor like an Indian trying to track buffalo. I was startled when I felt and heard heavy loud footsteps come in the room and walk right up to me. It was like someone was about to step on my head. I quickly sat up and questioningly scanned the room. A little shook up I ran into the room with my brother and sister to try and explain what had just happened. These were the kinds of things I would eventually write off as my imagination or some kind of elaborate misperception. They were unnerving, but not enough to make me lose any sleep at night.

My brother Eli was so young then, only four; he never really had to deal with the haunting on the level some of the rest of us did. Of course there were nights when he would get scared and come over to my room waking me up telling me someone was trying to get out of the small door in the corner of his room. I always blew these incidents off as being his overactive imagination and I would respond with my own imagination, magically making it ok for him to go back in his room and sleep. I remember one time we went in his room together when he was scared and surrounded his bed with little plastic cowboys and Indians that I told him would stand guard over his bed all night and keep him safe. This was enough peace of mind to get him back in his bed and asleep for the rest of the night. I regret ever having sent him back in that room to try and sleep those nights out alone but back then I simply didn't know any better.

My mother was always a working woman. It's almost as though she thrives on stressful positions where people depend on her to get the job done. She would experience about as much as Eli in the years we spent in the house. Often times I wish that she experienced more in the house because there is something that happens to your spiritual life and views on things that change so drastically when you have a supernatural experience. Experiencing the after life instead of talking about it makes it so real and puts your life into perspective in a way that you just can't explain to somebody and hope to achieve the same effect.

Now my sister Hannah was quite the different case. If I could relive all the events in the house from any family member's perspective I would definitely choose to relive them through the eyes and dreams of my sister. The physical as well as metaphysical things that she experienced are absolutely fascinating to me. The amazing thing is that I think she was only ever truly scared one or two times. She was always the hard-nosed my way or the highway type. I'd feel sorry for any ghost that ever tried to scare her out of her own room because it just won't happen. Hannah had a rare absolute lack of caring for what others thought of her that I believe was a direct result of her strong personal will. I hope more than anything that the extraordinary things she has experienced in the house will stay with her for the rest of her life. I hope that the immediate reality of our everyday lives doesn't creep into her memories and try to convince her that the things she saw were not real. In our lifetime there are few amazing moments that temporarily uncover small windows into the vastness and awesomeness of the world around us that we know not of from our daily routine. The window that she was allowed to look through was at times a shocking one that I am sure many people would have paid a lot of money to experience. But in the end she was chosen to be there and in the end I hope she takes what she has experienced and learns from it as I have.

My father was the first one to hear the sounds coming from upstairs. He was really the first to experience any kind of haunting at all, and really bore the brunt of it for the majority of the years. He was in his mid-thirties when we moved into the house; he had lived over three decades without ghosts being a reality in his life. I think this played a number on his mind when he would start to hear and see things in the house. On many occasions he would withhold these incidents from the rest of the family. I think he felt that since he was the only one experiencing these things on a weekly basis that maybe we would think he was going insane. He tells us now that often voices and faint sounds would enter his ear at night sounding like what he describes as an old time radio station being played. When he was explaining things to me that he had witnessed he would usually throw a, "Are we all just going crazy?!" in there. He was always the one to try and come up with a million different logical explanations of why these things were happening. Yet he could usually never find one satisfactory enough to convince him that what he experienced wasn't supernatural. Towards the last year, when the haunting got worse, he would begin to sense things in the house and be scared to death on a regular basis. At one point he was searching the house with a loaded colt .45 looking for an intruder that he swore he heard loudly enter through our backdoor. He would begin to regularly hear sounds coming from the upstairs. Often times he would feel as though someone were standing next to him or that an occasional presence would enter the room with him while he was alone. Whatever was in this house was attracted to my father for some reason. But, like my sister, I also hope that he doesn't convince himself with his overbearing logical view on life that the things he saw with his own eyes weren't really there.

I spent the first few weeks in the house checking over my shoulder out of paranoia and sleeping downstairs on the couch. The first thing I did after I found out the house was haunted was to go upstairs to my new room, where Emily supposedly spent most of her time, and tell her that I was scared to death and if she left me alone I'd leave her alone too. The worst was when I had to go in the basement at night to get a soda or something. The basement of the home is huge and I kept expecting to see a small girl in white standing in the corner staring at me. My already vivid imagination was really kicking in now and I was probably scaring the crap out of myself much worse than any ghost ever could. Luckily even though we were moving into our home in Edwardsville I still had two weeks of school to finish back in Columbia. I returned to stay with friends for a while, in the meantime trying to mentally prepare myself to come back and live in a haunted house. But as an eleven year old boy you don't really know how to mentally prepare for anything. At that point just being as far away from the house as I could get was good enough. My brother and sister went down to Kentucky to stay the two weeks during our transition with our grandparents. My Mom was to spend the first of the two weeks with me back in Columbia. This left my Dad in the house, for the first week, alone.....

Chapter Two

Making their presence known...

The first strange experience happened during my Dad's first week in the house. I think they were starting out small and working their way up; they didn't want to scare us out right off the bat. You probably just noticed that I said "they" instead of "she" but I'll get to that a bit later.

The first experience we ever had involved my Dad in the kitchen, cooking rice, when he suddenly had an urge to run upstairs and see if anything had moved around. He turned the gas flame on the stove down as low as it could go before running upstairs for the inspection. When he returned he immediately noticed the flame was turned all the way up. He walked over to turn the flame down and as he was adjusting the dial he felt a cold breeze pass by his legs. After hearing this, I was more scared than before, but when time came for me to leave everything I knew in Columbia and move into our Edwardsville home for good, I made the transition.

My family loves to collect antiques, particularly antique clocks. During the move the weights on the inside of one were jumbled up so badly that we gave up on ever getting it to work again. One day all five of us and our two dogs were in the basement cleaning up. Our biggest dog Yeti (he's the big white Great Pyrenees) was secured with a rope while we worked. He suddenly became very anxious and jumped up on his rope, choking himself and staring off into space. He whimpered and went on like this for a few minutes and we didn't think much of it. We emerged from the basement to grab some lunch and the old clock that had been broken since the move...chimed twice. Dad looked at Mom and immediately asked her if she had set the clock and she responded with a quick "no" and asked the same question to him. The time was actually two o'clock. Someone had set the clock to the exact time of day and was able to get it to work. The clock ran for about forty to forty five minutes then quit. Ever since that day we can wind the clock and it works just fine. We immediately phoned various family members about the incident and they advised trying to find out more about this Emily lady, and possibly getting some death records. My Dad obtained the abstract to our home and found out about Emily while investigating the city registry. The registry listed the names of the husband and wife for each year they lived in the house. There was a couple that had lived in the house during the early to mid 1900's. For every year there would appear two names, Joseph and Emma. The last entry that had Joseph and Emma's name was in 1950. Then the next year there was just Joseph, something had happened to Emily while living in the house. When our family got together that Christmas we went out to the cemetery to try and find Emily's grave. My uncle got out of the car and just started walking into the cemetery. A few seconds later he had found her grave, having walked right to it. We went on after that to get a copy of her death record. The death record said that Emily Raeber had been admitted to Highland hospital at two in the afternoon and pronounced dead of a brain aneurism about forty five minutes later. This discovery shed light on the clock incident and set a pattern of confusion followed by understanding that we experienced with the initially odd occurrences in the home.

So now this pretty well laid the foundation of what was really going on in our house, or so we thought. A woman named Emily had died while living in the house. After her death, her husband remained in the house for eleven years. Oddly enough he completely closed off the entire upstairs of the home while he lived there. I wonder… did he see his wife in the house after she died? Did he do something to her causing the fatal brain aneurism? I wonder if he could hear her up there dragging things across the floor at night like we did sometimes. Whatever it was, something caused this man to shut off the upstairs and try to put it as far from his mind as he could. After he had vacated the house entirely it was sold to Russell and Betty Davis. Betty was the one who sold it to us. She said when she bought the house the upstairs had been left to neglect for so long that you could literally see straight up through the roof in places where the rain had had its way.

Having grown the nerve to start sleeping upstairs, Emily was kind and let me be as I let her. I would spend the next eight years living in that room. I slept there every night feeling perfectly safe and comfortable as if I had never even been told my house was haunted at all. Nothing really ever happened to me in all that time to thoroughly convince me or scare me enough to believe without a doubt that there was somebody else in the room with me. But today, I'm back on the couch. I'll sleep upstairs sometimes but only in daylight. In fact it wasn't until I left the home for my first semester at college that I truly got a taste of the level of vivacious paranormal activity festering in my home. After what I went through, there hasn't been left a single thread of doubt as to the existence of Emily in my house. In fact, not just Emily, she was only the beginning.

As the years flew by and I grew up in the house, Emily was usually a quiet and subtle ghost that liked to play with things other than just the light switches. The occasional TV or radio coming on at full blast for a few seconds then shutting off were the kinds of electrical disturbances we would have in our house on a regular basis. Sometimes we would all look at each other and laugh when it happened. I used to have a computer in my room and at night the screen saver would come on a few minutes after I crawled in bed. This would cause the monitor to shut off until someone touched the mouse to wake it back up again. On many occasions I would be lying in bed a few minutes, after having turned out the lights, and I would hear the loud click of my monitor coming back to life. This meant there was some kind of electrical disturbance or someone had moved the mouse to my computer that caused the monitor to kick back on. I would open my eyes and scan the room as the light slowly grew from the screen and dimly illuminated everything around it. I was always so afraid that as things came into focus I would see somebody sitting in one of the chairs. I took this exact same computer to college for three years and never once has this happened.

One night my friend Justin and I had been in the room talking until about four in the morning. He was in a bed over by the closet doors and I was in my bed on the other side of the room. I switched off the light and we both rolled over. Just then I heard what I am sure was a voice but at the time I didn't hear what was said. After a few seconds of silence I asked, "Did you just say something?"

He responded, "Oh my God no! I was really hoping that was you because someone just said *goodnight*."

The buildup of all these little experiences didn't cause paranoia twenty four hours a day but my imagination could really take over and turn a normal experience into a nightmare. There was another occasion in the house that involved a loud booming storm outside just like in the movies. I was lying in my bed trying to get some sleep when I heard a faint tapping coming from the attic. The tapping grew louder and it seemed to be coming from the attic door. The room was pitch black with the occasional flash of lightning revealing images for only brief moments at a time. I reached over and desperately tried to flip on the lamp sitting at my bedside table. When I finally got the switch nothing happened, the storm had knocked out all the power to the house. By this time the tapping was growing even louder and was now on the floor between my bed and the door. In a bolt of wild anger, from being made to feel so scared by this ghost in my own home, I shot for the door. I stepped in something wet just feet before the doorway and immediately caught glimpses in my head of a pool of blood sitting there. I ran downstairs to get my dad who went in my room to investigate with a flashlight. He discovered that there was water, not the blood of a hundred tortured bodies, in the middle of my room. Apparently our old roof was having a hard time holding back the rain. The tapping had just been the journey of the leak from the attic to the floor. My paranoia really messed with my head sometimes but after all, can you really blame me?

One weekend my Dad was left alone in the house again while the rest of the family was out and about for various reasons. It was just him with the two dogs to keep him company. One of the nights he was in his bed trying to get to sleep when he heard someone hit a dead sprint and fly up the stairs to the second story. Startled, he glanced around the room to see both the dogs looking to him for some kind of guidance as to what should be done. Knowing that this wasn't an intruder and that Emily must have been playing tricks on him again, he tried the rest of the night to get some sleep, with one eye open of course.

We keep a large cast iron skillet on our stove at all times. We put it on the back burner so it wouldn't fall off and hurt anyone. In the middle of the night we heard it land in the pantry causing quite a loud noise and waking up most of the family. Someone had taken the skillet, moved it almost ten feet to the other side of the kitchen, and dropped it.

My Dad would always hear dragging noises across the floor in the upstairs of the house at night and during the day. One time I was in the house alone with a friend and we were working on a computer in the dining room. It was about one in the morning and we were cooking some pizzas. I started hearing very distinct thumping and dragging noises on the floor directly above our heads. Anticipating that this might be my first time seeing Emily I was pretty startled but glad to have my friend around even though he was just as scared as I was. The noises seemed to move into the upstairs hallway with an occasional squeak on the steps as the sounds seemed to be coming down to meet us. With a lot of courage and curiosity, I went into the kitchen and poked my head around the corner, looking up the stairwell to the second floor. There, in a heart pounding moment where I felt I was about to turn the corner and see this famous apparition that had been teasing and taunting my family for years, I saw nothing.

The best way I can describe these next experiences is that they were like some sort of a time warp. An example of this was one night when the whole family was in the living room watching a movie except me. I was in the bathroom when we all heard someone come in the back door and enter the kitchen. My friend, Daniel, is the only one allowed to enter the house in this fashion without knocking. He has always just walked in as though he is one of the family, so we all assumed he had just come in and it was no big deal. My Mom got up and went into the kitchen just to check, and I came out of the bathroom and entered the kitchen at the same time. No one was there. I called up to my room to see if Daniel was up there, but I got no response. Not five seconds later, he came walking in the back door. My Mom and I both stood there staring at him. We asked him if he just came in and left then came back in again. Confused, he said he hadn't and we all just went about the rest of the night wondering what had happened. It isn't uncommon to hear someone pull up in our driveway, go out to greet them, and have nobody there. But if you wait a few seconds sure enough they will come up the driveway. This is something for which we have yet to acquire any sort of explanation. Probably the worst instance of this was one winter when my Dad was back in the pantry putting away food from the grocery store. He turned to look out the back window at what sounded like a truck stuck in the snow spinning its tires, trying to claw its way to the road. Sure enough when he looked out the window he saw an antique style truck struggling in our neighbor's driveway. He walked back into the kitchen to get more groceries to put away. Seconds later he returned to the pantry and decided to look out the window again. What he saw was two cars, both covered in virgin snow. Utterly confused and questioning his own sanity it took him a while to relay to the family what he had experienced that day. Where that truck stuck in the snow came from, we may never know, but we do know there is something strange going on in this house.

These little occurrences continued to dot our lives as we lived in the home for the first several years. Up to this point nobody had actually seen Emily so we had no clue as to what she looked like. We just had a good idea of who she was. The longer we stayed there the more comfortable Emily became with us. The more comfortableshe became, the stranger things got.

Chapter Three

Reaching from the other side...

One of our more intense experiences came one night when we were all in bed except my parents. They were in the living room watching late night TV. Usually at that time my younger brother would have trouble sleeping and would come downstairs after being put to bed. Out of fear of being caught and sent back up to his room he would sneak downstairs and dwell in the kitchen or dining room until the inevitable sighting and order to return to his room. But this night was different, this night it wasn't my brother who was creeping around downstairs.

My Dad got up during a commercial to go to the kitchen. He had to cross through the dining room to get there and immediately caught someone out of the corner of his eye standing about two feet from him. This image was about the height of my little brother. My Dad assumed that's who it was and turned to confront him almost saying "Eli get back to bed." What my Dad saw instead of Eli was a short apparition standing within arms length. He described it as being a white see through figure on which it was very hard to make out any details. The figure started backing into the corner of the room alongside the dining room table and my Dad turned back to my Mom and said, "I think I just saw Emily." He then turned back and the apparition had somehow moved to the other side of the dining room table, backed up a little more and simply vanished before my Mom could get there to see anything. This wasn't an experience that my Dad would ever bring up or talk about in casual conversation, afraid that people might think he was crazy. This was the first time anyone had seen who we believe to have been Emily. Why she chose to reveal herself to him, at the time, we didn't know.

Not long before I left for my freshmen year at school we received a troubling message on our bathroom mirror. My

Mom was taking a shower one morning before work and when she got out she was startled to see the word HELP written on the glass. When she saw this she came upstairs and woke me up. When I got downstairs I looked in the misty mirror and sure enough the word "help" was there as though somebody had written it with their finger. I recreated the word on the following page exactly how it looked to us that day. The first two letters were very distinct while the last two seemed to start much higher on the mirror. Although it doesn't show in the recreation, the "L" and "P" seemed to fade as though there was less pressure used to create them. It was as if someone had been there in the bathroom for only a brief moment and quickly scribbled the message before being pulled away to somewhere else.

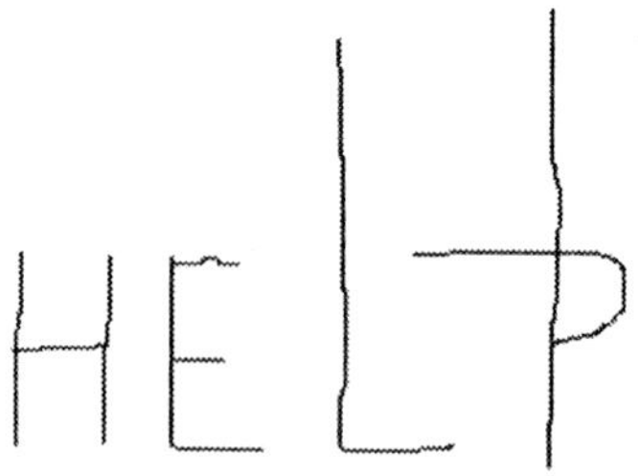

Help? Help from what? What did whoever wrote this want from us? Was Emily trying to tell us she was stuck here somehow and wanted help getting out? Did Emily even write it? Was my family collectively losing their minds? These were the kinds of things we would deal with and have to go about our day as if nothing was out of the ordinary.

Chapter Four

More than what meets the eye...

One thing we had tried in our house a few times before is the Ouija board. That's right, I'm talking about the little Parker Brothers game used to contact spirits for fun. One family reunion we all had a séance in the dining room with our Ouija board trying to contact Emily. At the time, it was just good family entertainment. Nothing happened when we did this. No monsters came leaping out of the table. Nobody became possessed with Emily's spirit and started talking in a low scary voice. It was just something we tried once for fun and then let it be as it showed no results.

When time came for me to move out of the house for college and head down to Murray State, I nervously left my hometown and made the transition. I was half excited about all the good times ahead for me in college and half scared of what it would be like. Much to my surprise when I got down there everybody was so friendly it made the transition almost effortless. I was to live in a dorm called Elizabeth College, a place full of liberal arts majors that more than made up in personality where we lacked desperately in athletic prowess.

What I didn't know about Murray State was that it was a Mecca of sorts for those involved in the occult. I met a lot of people in my dorm, many of whom were pagans. There was an organization on campus called SPA or Student Pagan Association. They would meet every Wednesday night and have a peaceful gathering except when they had to fend off invading Christians trying to make them "open their eyes to their sin." Needless to say this caused continual tension and arguing between the SPA Christian organizations on campus. It just so happened that two girls in my dorm, Stephanie and Becky, were active attendees of the SPA meetings and I became very good friends with them during my first few months. They would play around with occult stuff and sometimes I would watch for the entertainment. Other times I would just get bored with it and ignore whatever they were doing.

Becky was a shorter stocky girl with shoulder length curly hair that seemed to change colors about every week. The first few weeks in the dorm, every time I saw Becky she was usually sitting by herself in seclusion from the group of chattering students. I could tell she always kept an ear in what was being said because when people would make a joke I would glance over to see her reaction and she would be chuckling to herself.

Stephanie on the other hand was very loud and always restless. She would usually be in the middle of the conversation attracting the attention of the bystanders. She was a very pretty girl, thin with red hair and a strange accent that I could never quite place.

The two girls ended up becoming really good friends, they were completely inseparable and I would hang out with the two of them on occasion. Once Becky started to come out of her shell I found her to be great company. She was the quiet witty caring type and there was always this mysterious aura about her. Sometimes I would go up to her room or we would be hanging out somewhere together and not even have to say a word to each other. That's the way things were with Becky. I really don't know how to describe her except for the fact that when I was in a room with her I didn't have to say a thing and that was ok.

They started to get really involved with contacting spirits on the other side with the Ouija board that Becky brought from home. They claimed that the board Becky brought was blessed, so it was a much more effective tool for opening portals to the other side. They also explained to me that in order to actually get the board to work one of the participating members had to have what was called a "true belief." In other words they had to practically know it was going to work in the same way we may expect water to flow from a tap when we turn it on. The only one of us who had any experience doing things like this before was Becky. She had spent a lot of time contacting spirits through her board before she came to school. Although Stephanie had never done anything like this she seemed to possess a gift of psychic energy that allowed the spirits to work through her very effectively. So the result was Becky and Stephanie always operating the cursor on the board. I would have tried it a few times before it was all over but when I did it just moved too slowly and I became impatient. Plus I got really nervous when I did it and that didn't help. It was hard for me to relax and let go to what was happening.

One day I saw them down in the lobby of my dorm playing on the board and laughing so I went over to see what they were doing. It was interesting to watch how the curser flew around the board and I was trying to figure out how they made it do that yet keep their fingers just barely touching. Being totally skeptical at first I asked a lot of stupid questions and was basically being a smartass. They said they were talking to someone on the board named JT. JT went on to tell us about how his friend murdered him in a river and his body was never found. He told us that he did it because he and his friend Zack were fighting over who would get his "mamma's" house when she died. JT said they were both drunk and started yelling. Then Zack hit JT on the head with a rock and knocked him out. JT's body fell into the water and Zack left his body in the water to drown.

At the time this all seemed like quite an elaborate prank the girls had put on attempting to trick me and I wondered how much time they had spent rehearsing. But the personality on the board seemed to take its own shape the longer we talked. Becky and Stephanie were very nonchalant about the whole thing and I became very interested in JT's life on the other side. I would try to come up with ways I could test him to be sure it wasn't just these girls playing a trick on me. Remembering about my haunted house back home, I got an idea.

I asked JT to go to my house, find out what is on the license plates of all our cars, and then come back. I decided to have him do this because it was a way for me to have him go to my house without the expectation of spirits being there. So JT left and about an hour later we came back and sure enough as soon as the girls touched the board he was there.

JT began to tell me that there were two people in the house when he visited. He told me about how many cars were in the driveway but I was unimpressed. I asked him if he saw anybody there like himself. He said yes. I asked if it was a boy or a girl. He said girl. I asked what her name was. I was floored when I saw what name was being spelled out on the board...EMILY. I couldn't believe it! Now I was hooked, I wanted more information! I wanted to know how he knew that! He said that Emily was upset because there was a man in the garage who was being "terrible." Confused and excited at the same time I wanted to know more about JT's visit to my house.

A little background before I go on about our garage. A few years before this my Dad and I had raked a guy's yard and he gave us a green 1963 Ford Fairlaine for our efforts. Little did we know at the time there was a reason we received the car for so little.

JT said that Emily was upset because there was a guy in our garage named Stan who was "really bad" and would try to hurt my family. I asked JT if he saw any cars in the garage and he said yes. I asked him what color. He said green. I asked him what brand and he said Ford. JT would spell "Abe no cars" over and over again on the board. He said he was too scared of Stan to get close enough to read the license plates. Then he would go back to spelling "Abe no cars" again. I had to calm him down because he was so upset about Stan that he never wanted to go back. Just like a house can be haunted, so can a vehicle, we now had both. Stan must have been the reason why we were able to obtain the car so easily in the first place.

I wanted JT to go back and get Emily so I could talk to her. He said that he would do it but that he really didn't want to and, no matter what, he wasn't going back in the garage to deal with Stan. As I sent him back to get Emily, I was incredibly excited to be on the verge of talking to a dead woman who had been with me for the past eight years watching me grow up. I felt as though I already knew her before she even came to talk to me. A few seconds later JT returned with Emily.

Talking to her on the Ouija board her first concern was for me and a relationship with a girl I had down at school. She told me that I needed to break up with her because she was evil and wasn't any good for me. I was already thinking about doing it anyway because I knew deep down that it was not a positive thing. I actually ended up sharing everything Emily said with my girlfriend at the time before I broke up with her. I guarantee she never had a breakup excuse like that before and I doubt she'll soon forget it.

Asking Emily if there was anything we could do for her in the house, she was excited to ask me to plant more flowers for her in our yard. She said she really loved tulips and it would be great if we could plant some for her. Also, she told us that she had appeared to my Dad in the dining room once because "he is good, and he can help with the flowers." She said she wanted Stan out of the garage because he was "terrible and would hurt the family". This was the reason she wrote HELP in the mirror. She was trying to get our attention to get rid of the Fairlaine because it brought Stan to us and it could take him away. When I asked her why she was still in the house she said she was there to protect the family. She wanted me to tell everybody "hi" for her and also wanted to know why my Dad took all the pictures down in his room. My Dad is a professional photographer and for some reason he had started taking down all the pictures in his room and only had a few left. Becoming more and more convinced, I was getting very excited and wanted to spread the news to my family.

Ecstatic, I called home trying to relay all the things I had just found out in about one breath. I think my parents were a little confused as to what was happening at first but they gave me more things to ask Emily to verify that it was really her and that these girls weren't just playing tricks. After what I had seen there was no doubt in my mind that what was happening was well beyond the ability of these girls. They weren't capable of knowing all that stuff about my house and my family to fabricate it into a huge game for fun. But, understandably so, my parents wanted more proof so I set out to get it. That night I went to a party off campus and returned to the dorms a few hours later. I went upstairs to the girls' room and both of them were up there just hanging out. As soon as I walked in the room I wanted to get back on the Ouija board and talk to Emily again. Of course the first person we got was JT as he seemed to always be there when we first got on. He told us never to use the board unless they knew he was present to keep "bad things from coming through." We agreed and I asked him a few questions about talking to other people who had died. He said when people die they either stay here or go "high." I asked him if he could talk to people who had gone high and he said he wasn't able to do that yet. JT hadn't been a ghost for very long and like anything else the longer you do something the better you get at it. Since JT had only been dead for about ten years, he was able to do some things but was still learning a lot about existing on the other side.

I have had three big dogs in my life that grew up with me ever since I was little. All three have passed away and they were each like brothers to me. At this particular time it had just been six months since the last of my big dogs, Yeti, died. That's one of the reasons I wanted to know about JT contacting spirits that have died and gone high. I just wanted to know if my dogs were living on beyond this life somehow like JT was. This is what was in the back of my mind that night as I talked to Emily and JT on the Ouija board.

I eventually got around to asking JT to go back to my house and get Emily so I could talk to her again. He left and a few seconds later he returned with her. She immediately took the main seat at the board and I began talking to her. Emily is a no nonsense kind of spirit. She hates to be out of the house and when she is she doesn't like to play around. I had started off asking a few general questions for small talk and to get to know her a little better but she almost left. So I got right down to what I wanted to do. I asked her why she never did anything to me in the last eight years I was living there and she replied, "Abe scared." She was glad that I wasn't afraid of her anymore and asked if it would be ok if she came to me in my dream that night. I told her that would be fine because I wanted to know what she looked like anyway. Then I asked her if she could move something in the room. She said she could and she would, but she would wait until we all least expected it. I left the room for a few minutes to go get something from my room and when I got back the girls had an exciting story to tell about how a shelf had fallen over while I was gone. When we got back on the board I asked Emily why she waited until I had left to do anything and she said that for me she was going to wait till I was alone to move something.

Then I told her that my parents wanted more proof that I was really talking to her so I asked if I could ask her some questions and the cursor pointed to "ok." I asked her to tell me about some of the pictures we have in our house on the walls. She told me about one of Hannah, my sister. She told me there were a few of me and one of Dusty, our late golden retriever. She was totally right about all of this except the picture she thought was of Dusty was actually of Duke, a dog of ours that had died before we ever even moved to Edwardsville. But seeing as how both Dusty and Duke were both Golden Retrievers it was understandable how she would confuse the two. I asked her if she could contact any of the dogs for me and she said "yes." She said she could contact Dusty and Yeti but that Duke had gone "too high." My heart began racing as my main motive for the night was to see if I could actually speak to Yeti. I started out with Dusty, asking her to contact him for me. Then speaking for Dusty she spelled out "good dog wants Abe" on the board. For some reason at that moment I was totally overwhelmed by everything and almost lost it. Knowing that my dogs were still alive, that there was an afterlife, and that there was so much going on around us all each day that we have no comprehension of just hit me all at once. I started to break down crying, yelling, totally confused and shocked all at the same time about what was going on. I decided not to contact Yeti because it was just too much at the time. Later that night I went to my room and wrote a long email to my family about what was happening to me at school. That night I hit my pillow and practically blacked out remembering nothing from my dreams at all. This all happened on a Wednesday night, remember that.

Chapter Five

Beginning to take hold...

The next day when I woke up my roommate told me that I was freaking him out in my sleep. He said, "The boogieman was after you or something" and that I was moaning and thrashing around in my bed. A little alarmed by this it bothered me for a while but I soon just seemed to forget about it. Exactly what happened that night I probably won't know for a very long time, but that night there was a spiritual awakening for me. In my sleep something happened in the spiritual world that was the beginning of a small series of visions to a friend of mine that would later change my life. A friend who was back home in Edwardsville who knew next to nothing about what was going on with me down at school.

I began to spend a lot of time talking with JT. I was fascinated by the idea that I had a contact on the other side, a contact that I was beginning to call my friend. I wanted all the answers to life's biggest questions. I wanted to know about reincarnation, aliens, past lives, abortion, but it was odd because what later became my obsession I never even thought to ask about. God never once came up in any of our lengthy conversations. I would spend my time in class coming up with more questions for JT and then come back to the dorms that night and spend hours talking to him. He seemed to know everything there was to ever know about everyone. He knew that one of the girls who was in the room with us used to tell her teachers her name was Dorothy when she was in first grade because she didn't want them to know her real name. It was as though he had watched the movie of my whole life and taken really good notes. He knew the name of the first girl I ever kissed in sixth grade back in Columbia, Missouri. JT would tell me that at night he would come to me in my dreams and we would laugh a lot and share stories. The way I would share a story with him would be to simply remember the incident. Then he could just watch it as I remembered it. It was the most effective way I have ever shared an experience with anybody in my entire life. He was able to see situations exactly as I saw them and feel the same way I did. Because we communicated in this manner we were able to break the boundaries that limited traditional communication. Instead of speaking to him through words about how I felt about something I could just give him the feeling. Sharing in this way taught me a lot about the limits our language places on our ability to really communicate. Have you ever been talking to someone and felt they really understood where you were coming from? Like you really connected with them because the abstract concepts you were trying to convey with words got across to the other person with beautiful clarity. Some believe those moments of contact are what we live for. That's the way it was with JT all the time and because of it we grew really close really fast.

Up to this point I had never even touched the board. The girls did most of the communication since they seemed to be more comfortable with their spiritual abilities. They had been working to develop their abilities to communicate with the other side for some time and were much better vessels than I was. Each time I would try and use the board with one of them the cursor would go very slowly because I couldn't relax. It was always blowing my mind so much when it was happening that I would become tense. I do remember the first time JT moved something using my energy. I was in the kitchen of a friend's house and I made a makeshift Ouija board on the kitchen counter with two glasses and a bottle cap. I touched the bottle cap and asked JT if he was there and told him to go ahead and move the cap if he was. It moved a little bit but nothing convincing. Then I tried to relax a little more and the cap just shot up to the glass that was representing yes on the counter.

I had a job at the front desk of my dorm that was extremely boring. I would have to sit down there for hours on end. While I was doing all this at school I found a small plastic butterfly and used to practice moving it with JT on the counter at the desk. Of course nobody ever knew what I was doing. It probably just looked like I was just bored and playing with this little butterfly because I had nothing better to do. I never did get good enough to use the Ouija board because the girls were usually there and it worked so much better when they were on it. It was for this reason that I had planned to bring them home with me. Besides, my parents wanted to see this first hand and JT and Emily were very excited about being able to communicate with the family. I had family coming down from Wisconsin and other parts of Illinois with whom I wanted to share this experience. I had even asked JT to spend time with them so that when we used the board he would know things about them that we could use to help prove he was real.

Another strange thing that started happening was that I started finishing JT's responses on the board before he could spell out even a few letters. He would start to spell something and I would just say what I felt he was trying to convey, then he'd point to yes. It was like I was talking to him in my head and feeling his thoughts in my mind. I sat in silence talking to JT in my head while he responded to me on the board. The girls would keep touching the cursor and it would move as JT and I had our conversation but I never spoke a word. It got to the point where the girls became frustrated when JT and I talked like this because they never knew what we were talking about.

Stephanie and Becky didn't know that I had been a civil war re-enactor with my Dad for a few years before I came down to Murray. I had always had a strange obsession with the confederate flag. Ever since I was young I had a huge one hanging in my room. I never knew why I liked the flag so much except that I just thought it was really cool.

Asking about reincarnation one night JT told me that I was a general in a past life, a general in the civil war. Not just any general but my life long military hero Stonewall Jackson. He also told me that my Dad had been with me in the war as a private in my army and sometimes I would ride to find him amongst the troops and we would talk as the army moved from place to place. JT told me that I was shot and killed in the battle of Antietam by my own men, which is exactly how I thought Stonewall died. He said that my Dad was also shot and killed in the battle of Antietam while trying to save a friend on the field. After all that, JT proceeded to explain to me that I was a special spirit sent down to earth when something big was supposed to happen. He said my Dad serves as a helper to get me to accomplish what I am supposed to do. The day that I found all this out my Mom and Dad just happened to be out in Washington D.C. on a business trip. I called to tell them all the crazy new things I had found out. When I asked them to take a wild guess at who I was a reincarnation of my Dad said Stonewall much to my surprise. "How did you know that?!" I exclaimed and he said that just that morning he had been standing next to a statue of Stonewall at Bull Run thinking about how awesome it was to be in the same place Stonewall once stood.

At the time I was being told this I honestly believed that Stonewall had died at Antietam. But upon further research done months after that day I found out that he died at Chancelorsville. This serves as a perfect example of how sometimes the spirits on a Ouija board will make up stuff and tell you whatever you want to hear to keep you hooked. I wasn't sure if this meant that *all* the things they told me on the Ouija board were lies or not, but as for this particular bit of information I knew it had to be false.

JT also told me I was once a woman named Betty Page and for the longest time I had no idea who this person was. At school some early copies of my book were beginning to circulate around campus. One night I got a call from a classmate and she told me she knew who Betty Page was. Betty Page actually has her own website. She had lived as a famous personality that spent some time as a Playboy centerfold in the 1950's. This was just another odd thing the spirits told me on the board whose truth I don't think I can ever know.

With my parents in Washington and me in Kentucky my brother and sister were staying in the house with my grandparents. The more I seemed to talk to the spirits on the board, the stranger things seemed to get, both in Kentucky, and back home.

Chapter Six

Something stirring in the shadows...

At this point I was spending a lot of time talking with the spirits. One thing I've always used as verification that I was in fact talking to someone or something on the board, that was from my house, is the stuff that started happening back home to my sister. When I moved out my sister moved into my old room, one of the rooms in the house that Emily likes to spend a lot of time in. While all this was going on, I would call home frequently but I would only tell my parents what was going on. They chose not to tell my brother and sister much because they didn't want to scare them. My sister Hannah began to have a lot of strange things happen to her. She told me that she would wake up in the middle of the night standing in the corner of her room holding a picture of a woman that she had taken off her wall. She also said that she would have this reoccurring dream where she met a woman she had never seen before. The dream went something like this... My sister and my Dad stepped off the back porch of our home heading to the garage. As my sister approached the garage she noticed a white object running down the alley behind the garage. She would also see a cat that usually appeared on the roof of the garage somewhere. My sister looked up and noticed a woman dressed in white with really long sleeves standing next to the garage. She felt as if she knew the woman and was not alarmed by her presence at all. When Hannah got close to the garage the woman would stop her and tell her not to enter. The woman even grabbed her hands at one point and made her promise never to go in the garage alone. The lady told my sister that if she went into the garage something bad would happen. She even went as far as to explain to her that my dad would tell her to get something out of the Fairlaine and when she got in the car to get it she would be locked in and suffocated to death. She had the dream about five times and every time it would progress a little further. At the farthest point of its progression Hannah would find herself walking around to the side of the garage after encountering the woman. Then she would find out what the white thing was running in the background. Our dog Yeti was there with a full, bright white set of hair. He would walk up to Hannah in her dream and she would remember that he was dead, start crying, then wake up.

Yeti had a role in this whole story. It's almost as if he was always there with us, protecting us. Always being in the background, not really noticeable in the main plot of what was going on but always present as a guardian of sorts. I think people have a much stronger connection with their animals than they ever realize. I think our pets are intelligent beings with a strong sense of love for their families. Yeti was our guard dog when he lived with us, always on the alert when someone entered the house or strayed too close to our yard. It would seem that even though he has gone from the physical world he still remains with us and ever watchful from a distance.

Along with these dreams Hannah actually had a very short yet intense experience of a miniature spiritual battle though she had no idea what it was at the time. Hannah was upstairs lying on her bed trying to fall asleep one night. She had a soda on her bedside table. She tried to lean up to grab her soda when she realized she couldn't move her arm. She tried to sit up but all she could do was pick up her head. Realizing her body was pinned down on her bed she picked up her head to look around. She put her head back down on the pillow, then picked it up a few seconds later now becoming very scared. When she did this she realized that the picture on her wall of the woman, the same picture she found herself holding when she would wake up in the middle of the night, had somehow come off the wall and was now on her chest. A few seconds later she felt hair go across her face and the force lifted.

Hannah never seemed to be that frightened by all of what was going on. Despite these strange encounters she was experiencing she continued to sleep upstairs alone. This has always amazed me because I know if I were living up there and half of the stuff that happened to her would have happened to me, I would have been on the couch in a heartbeat. Yet her stubbornness kept her in place and steadfastly determined to keep her room. When I called her she was very confused at the time wanting to know why she couldn't go in the garage alone and why all these strange things were going on. I explained to her that I thought the lady in her dreams was Emily. As for the picture, and being pinned down in her bed, I had no idea. So I turned back to the board for answers.

JT's "mamma" started to get sick and he wanted to spend his time with her instead of talking to us. It was very hard to get him to come through for more than a minute or two. For some reason if we didn't have JT to go get Emily we couldn't seem to summon her. Wanting desperately to know what was happening at my house we tried to get Emily on the board without JT's help. One night Stephanie and I sat down to use the board by ourselves. We sat there with the cursor motionless and tried to contact Emily. Soon a sort of heaviness filled the room and the cursor started to move very slowly and spell out things that didn't make any sense. It would run off the board frequently and made for frustrating communication. Stephanie and I decided then would be a good time to get the hell out of there and we did. We went outside down to the "amp," a little miniature concrete amphitheater out front of the dorm. We were out there alone and felt as though the thing had followed us. But after a while it lifted and we went back to the room. We tried to contact JT again and he was there. We asked him what had happened and he told us that we should have never tried to contact Emily without him. He said that what came through to us while he was gone was something bad. We agreed never to use the board again unless JT was there. JT then told us that Zack was doing something to his Mom to make her sick. JT wanted me to go stop Zack from hurting his "mamma." But he soon caught himself in his plea and decided to keep quiet.

In the spirit world there are rules and laws just like we have here. Except, I think the enforcers of those laws are much more powerful and knowing than the police in our world. For JT to tell us what we can do to get him out of his perpetual state or to have us actually do something to alter a course of events that we normally wouldn't be involved in is breaking some kind of law. Emily was the same way. When I would ask her how we could help her move on she would immediately leave.

An example of this with Emily had to do with that suspicious wall in our basement. One family reunion we were going to knock that wall down for entertainment, but for some reason we didn't. I asked Emily about this incident and she said it had made her very nervous. She would stop and not want to talk about it anymore. To this day I believe that if we were to knock down that wall we would find something. I don't know what, but it might be one of the pieces in the puzzle of why there are spirits in our home.

Getting back to JT and his sick mother, it was taking all his time and he was spending less and less with us. One night I tried talking to him just in my head quietly, sending him encouraging words to help him deal with his situation. The next day when I talked to him on the board he said that he had heard me and he was feeling better about the whole thing. He was back, in higher spirits than he had been, and he was willing to go get Emily for me so I could find out what the heck was going on at my house. He left and soon Emily was with us on the board. I immediately asked her if she was coming to my sister in her dreams and she said yes. She said she was trying to protect her from Stan the best she could. I then asked her about the picture of the lady and Emily said simply, "Hannah is pretty and the picture is pretty so I thought Hannah should have the picture." I then wanted to know about Hannah being pinned down in her bed. Emily said that when that happened Stan was actually in the house trying to hurt Hannah. Emily, her cat Roger, and a nice man who sometimes came to the house were surrounding Hannah to protect her from Stan. Emily said that the hair Hannah felt on her face was Roger walking past her. I asked Emily about her cat and she said she kept him around to keep her company.

We once had a garage sale at my house and a middle aged man showed up claiming to have once lived in the house. He said he was Betty Davis' son and had grown up there. He was excited to be back at his childhood home so we invited him in. While we were giving him the tour we got to the kitchen and he stopped. He went into a story about how he and his Dad were working out in the yard and they came in for lunch. He said his Dad, Russell Davis, just passed out and died in the kitchen of a brain aneurism, which, if you remember, is the same thing that caused Emily's death. The best explanation I can offer for the "nice man" that Emily said helped her fight off Stan is that he was Mr. Davis.

Armed with answers I called home and let them know what I had found out from Emily about the things that were going on there. I spent that same night with the girls and JT on the board talking late. We were talking about aliens and laughing till we were practically crying. JT had a great sense of humor. I loved spending time with JT and we were teaching each other so much.

Chapter Seven

The visions...

As I was going through this whole week I was so enthralled with what I was doing that I neglected to read any of the emails from my friends back home. One of my friends had sent me two emails and one was about to drop off the bottom of my list so I figured I should read it soon. It was entitled "dreaming about you." This was an email my friend Katie wrote as a result of a dream that she had. She had it on Wednesday night, the same night I experienced my awakening while talking to Emily on the Ouija board the same night trying to contact Yeti and the same night I supposedly thrashed in my sleep. The email was simple and to the point. She described a dream where I was sitting by a river crying my eyes out with my head buried in my hands. She said Yeti was sitting next to me licking my face trying to make me feel better. Seeing as how Katie was dreaming about me and my dead dog on the same night I was trying to contact him my interest was immediately triggered. I became a little nervous as I clicked on her second email called "Dreaming about you again." The following is the actual email, unedited, exactly how I read it that day, an email that would have a tremendous impact on the rest of my life.

this is kinda weird cause i dont think i've ever had any serious dreams about you before, and i usually don't have them at all but i had another one last night. bare with me. i was debating about telling you about this one cause it just seems dumb and i know you think i'm a religious fanatic (which i am honestly far from) but i wanted to tell you. and to be honest with you, i've heard something is up with you. not sure what though. WRITE TO ME DAMNIT! k, here it is. it was pretty short. it was you and me sitting by this river again and you were upset and crying and i was trying to console you. i had my arm around you and after awhile you turned your head away from me and started talking to someone who i couldn't see. then all the sudden god's presence was there and he was pissed. he said to read the last two pages of the bible and that a bridge needed to be built over a garden???? yeah, so that's that. i dont know if that means anything to you or my imagination is running wild. i hope everything is ok and if i'm way dumb, just delete this and we'll pretend that nothing happened. cool? take care of yourself, see ya soon, kt ps: i did look at the last two pages of the bible. weird shit. i'm clueless. i got nuthin...

Absolutely shocked at what I was reading I almost started to panic and immediately ran downstairs to a friend's room to get a Bible. I flipped open to the last two pages of the Bible and in Revelation 21:8 it reads "But cowards, traitors, perverts, murderers, the immoral, **those who practice magic**, those who worship idols, and all liars—the place for them is the lake burning with fire and sulfur which is the second death." Needless to say I was scared to death. God, whom I never even knew existed, just burst onto the scene and to top it off he was mad at me, making me feel like a complete reprobate for what I had done. It's not a good feeling to know that God is mad at you. I cried, I called my Mom and Dad to tell them what had happened, I swore off the Ouija board, and I prayed and asked forgiveness over and over. The next morning when I woke up and walked out of my dorm I was shocked to see a handful of Gideons passing out free Bibles. Taking it as an obvious sign and beckoning from God I took two and asked one of the elders if I could speak with him about my situation. That afternoon I went and met with him at his office spilling everything I had done in the last week. He told me that what I did was wrong and dangerous. He said that depending on how much control the "demons" had on me, the harder and more torturous it would be to get out. Scared to death I went back to my room and read from the Bible, placing one under my pillow and praying before I went to sleep that night and every night until I got baptized. I wouldn't even go to class without at least one Bible in my pocket at all times.

I had some good explanations for why Yeti, Katie, JT and God were in Katie's dreams but I didn't understand what the riverbank was all about. I was sitting out front of Elizabeth on a park bench when one of the girls who lived there with me asked why I looked so worried. I had talked to her recently about the activities I was involved in on the Ouija board so I just went right in to telling her about Katie's dreams. She told me she had a dream book up in her room I could use if I wanted to. At this point I was open to anything so I went to her room with her and we looked up riverbank in the book. It said a riverbank symbolizes "A close proximity to a spiritual search or awakening."

That next weekend was the weekend I had planned to bring Stephanie and Becky to my home with me to use the

Ouija board in my house with the visiting relatives. I felt like the spirits, especially Emily, were upset with me for suddenly cutting off all communication with them. When I came home from school my sister woke up the next morning and found our family Ouija board, that we usually keep in the basement, under her bed. I felt like Emily was obviously reaching out to me and wanted to talk to the family. I can remember her saying she had something to tell my Dad but wanted to wait until we were all in the house and she could do it more privately. When I was in the house I expected to see Emily every time I turned around. I felt like she was always standing there watching me, trying desperately to get my attention. Despite this, I remained steadfast from the Ouija board and was baptized by my grandfather that weekend along with my brother and sister.

We ended up planting a hundred tulips in the yard for Emily, sold the haunted Fairlaine and our house finally felt at peace. But what we didn't know was that this story was far from over.

Soon after my baptism my friend had a third dream about me. It was very short, simple, and to the point. She saw me standing in a white place all alone. God came down behind me and did what she described as a "signing of his name on my back." That was all she saw in her dream but for me to hear that was very relieving and encouraging, and affirming that I was now on the right path.

At that time my relationship with God began to grow and it was a wonderful thing. Coming to know a lot about God and my purpose in this world was a very enlightening experience for me and even though it was scary at times I thank God for the awakening and awareness he has blessed me with at such a young age. The whole thing really helped me to realize what is important in my life and prioritize my daily activities, thoughts, and relationships to help prepare myself for whatever it is that God wants me to do. I think at this point, above all else, it is just that he wishes that I come to know and recognize him and to eventually reach the point where I want nothing more but to abide in his spirit.

Chapter Eight

Something left unfinished...

At first I didn't really tell many people about everything that had happened to me because I thought they would just pass me off as a kid looking for attention. I can remember one of the first times I told the story to a friend. I had sat my friend Fish down in his room and told him everything with the door closed while there was a party going on in the rest of the house. We were back there for hours and when I was almost done with the story his friend Mike came knocking on the door. Mike is a big fraternity guy who, at the time, was the president of the Sigma Chi's down at school. When we opened the door Mike had this horrified look on his face like he just saw a ghost. We invited him in and he started crying and he told us he was just walking out of the bathroom next to our room and sensed something in the shower, something so powerful and real it practically put him in a state of shock. I don't know what was lurking outside the room that night either listening or trying to break up our conversation, but whatever it was, it was enough to scare the hell out of somebody that didn't even know what was going on.

Things from then on were pretty quiet for a while. Sometimes Hannah would see her closet doors, turn away for a few seconds, then look back and they would be open. Sometimes she would get home from school and they would be open when she had closed them before she left. This didn't seem to scare her much and she would just close them back and go about her day. One night Hannah was in her room and she just happened to glance over at her doorway while scanning the room for something. She actually caught a glimpse of someone in the doorway when she was scanning over it and immediately turned back to look and see what it was. Whatever it was she saw was gone and shortly after she heard the beads that hung on her door gently rattling as if someone had just passed through.

The next time I saw my sister after I went back for my spring semester at school was during Easter at my grandparent's house. That night she had a very strange dream. She dreamt that she was at my aunt's house in Florida and my whole family was there. She was playing outside when Emily showed up in the yard, hanging on to Yeti by his collar. Hannah said that Yeti looked strange to her because his head was smaller than usual making him disproportionate in shape. She said Emily then spoke to her saying, "don't be afraid." In the dream she became scared and ran into the house and into a room where our parents were asleep. When she got there she jumped in bed with my Mom and latched onto her while looking back at the door she entered through, waiting for Emily to follow her. When she saw nothing she looked back at my Mom who had now become Emily! Emily was holding onto Hannah and had Yetis collar in one of her hands and she again repeated the words "don't be afraid." When I heard about this I immediately knew that Emily was trying to reach out to us again and communicate. Emily didn't want us to be afraid of her but in our minds was the possibility that the spirits were demons or something that we shouldn't have been messing with. Understandably we also thought God was mad at me for talking to her and JT. I still had a lot of unanswered questions from the Ouija board experience but I was still too scared to touch the board again. When I was home I would pray for God's will to be done in the house and once even blessed the rooms with oil.

When I came home for the summer I had my friend Fish stay with me for the first few days. We had to stay in the room Eli grew up in because Hannah was now in my old room. I went back to sleeping upstairs every night and was doing just fine without getting too freaked out. One of the first nights after my friend left to go back to school I had to stay in my new room all by myself. I woke up around three in the morning and immediately had a strange feeling as I looked around the room. I tried lying my head back down to fall back asleep as soon as possible. A little while after I did that I thought I felt something touching my foot that was hanging off the end of the bed. I immediately opened my eyes and may have seen something at the end of my bed but, seeing as how I had been sleeping, I brushed it off as my eyes being tired. Still a little alarmed I got out of bed and began turning on lights in the room. I stood out in the hallway for a second and started hearing faint voices but I couldn't make out what was being said. I went into my sister's room and she was asleep on her bed. What made my blood jump was that her closet door was standing wide open the way Emily always left it when she would open it. I got my stuff and went downstairs. In the morning I asked my sister if her closet door was opened when she went to bed and she said no. From then on I was on and off sleeping up there at night. Usually coming in really late at night and having to go up there when everybody else in the house was already asleep made staying upstairs a lot harder. I wanted so much to believe that the last chapters with Emily had been written and I no longer had anything to worry about but before my family could close the book on this story there was still something left unfinished.

Chapter Nine

A visitation...

One day in the summer a week or two later, I found an old incense burner on a shelf in my house. I asked my Dad if he had any incense for it and he gave me some frankincense and myrrh from a small basket above the wine rack. I burnt it and it was very strong filling up the whole house with its powerful aroma. What I didn't know about this stuff is that Abraham used to use it in the Bible to ward away evil and attract angels. Well, what happened that night whether it was something good or bad we can't tell for sure. But what did happen I believe was in part a reaction to burning this incense in my home.

That night I woke up again at about three something feeling very hot and uncomfortable. I seemed to be wide awake as if I hadn't even been asleep at all. I could tell something was really wrong and got my stuff to head downstairs immediately. I gathered up my blanket and pillows and stepped into the hallway. I opened my sister's door and saw that she was still on the computer in her room with all her lights out. I didn't hear her say anything to me as I turned and walked down the stairs through the kitchen and into the living room where I sat on the couch. I immediately became tired again and tried to go to sleep. A few seconds after I laid down, I heard a loud cat meow but seeing as how our windows were open that night I dismissed it as coming from outside. That's all I remember from that night but what happened upstairs just minutes after I left has kept me from sleeping up there since.

My sister said that she heard the same cat meow that I did except she heard it distinctly outside of her bedroom door. She turned around thinking that a cat had somehow sneaked up there and she grabbed her phone in a panic to use as a weapon if needed. She didn't see anything when she turned around but soon heard the meow again and looked to the bottom of her door. Sure enough sitting right there was what she described as the scariest thing she had ever seen in her life! A huge golden cat with matted up hair was sitting there looking straight at her practically meowing so loud she said it sounded like screams. Hannah started screaming "oh my God, oh my God" in total fear as the cat advanced towards her chair. The cat walked right up to the chair and sat down on the floor while continuing to stare directly at Hannah. She then saw a soft blue light emanate from the corner of her room that attracted her attention. She said near the small door entering her closet was a woman standing about four and a half to five feet tall. Hannah said she looked like a real person; she had her left arm up against her body like one would hold a broken arm in a sling. Her right arm was down towards the floor and holding a flower. Hannah described the person as having a young face on either an older woman's body or a burnt body. She said the woman was in all white and in the face looked just like the woman in her dreams. Totally paralyzed in fear, Hannah now looked back at the cat that was scaring her the most then looked back up at the woman again. When she looked back up after having taken her eyes off the woman for but a split second she was startled to see the woman had halved the distance of the room towards her and was now standing about five feet from her. Also, the cat had somehow joined the woman, now next to her arching its back and hissing loudly. Hannah said the wind from her fan was gently blowing the woman's hair. The woman stood and stared at Hannah for a whole minute which seemed like an eternity. Hannah described the woman's face as looking like a dead person with their eyes open. She said the woman's eyes weren't just open they were wide open and she also had her mouth slightly ajar with her head cocked to one side. After a minute of this awkward stare down, Hannah said she blinked and the woman was gone. The bizarre thing is that this happened just minutes after I left the upstairs, otherwise I may have seen it too. Something awakened me and the bad sense I got about the room was very real. If I heard the first cat meow then why didn't I hear Hannah's screams when she initially saw the cat in her room? All I can figure is somehow something was keeping her screams from being heard anywhere else in the house. Also, when I initially left my room and started walking downstairs Hannah said she saw me in her doorway and when I turned to go down the stairs she asked me where I was going. I didn't respond because even at that point just within feet of her doorway I was not able to hear anything coming from the room.

Now I was seriously freaked out to be in my house. Even my sister who had been through quite a lot refused to sleep in the upstairs for the first few nights after the incident. We knew something had to be done about this and fast. We had no clue what was going on in our house and honestly we didn't know who to turn to for help. I had prayed for my house many times but this didn't seem to have any effect. Needless to say we were scared and very confused.

Chapter Ten

Searching for help...

The next day we called Betty Davis, the woman who sold us the home, and told her about some of the things that had been happening but not everything because that would have taken hours. She was shocked to hear that there ever was a woman who had once lived in the house and died there named Emily. She just always thought her daughter made that name up. She also said that she used to stay in the room Hannah was currently in with her husband and they would see Emily walk out of those closet doors all of the time. She told us that we should call her daughter because she had the most contact with Emily and would love to hear about what she was doing in the house. We told her we found out about Emily dying around two something in the afternoon of a brain aneurysm. She immediately pointed out the parallel of her own husband also dying in the kitchen at approximately the same time of day and from the same thing.

We were able to contact Betty's daughter, Cara, later that week and eagerly told her about what had been happening at the house. It's odd; she described Emily as being nothing like the woman Hannah saw in her room. And she knew nothing about Emily ever having a cat.

Another odd inconsistency is that Emily died when she was seventy two. The woman Hannah had seen looks much younger than that. Emily used to tell me on the Ouija board that she would appear to Hannah much younger than she actually was as not to frighten her. But why then would she only alter her face and not the rest of her body when doing this? The whole thing just didn't make much sense to me. When Hannah saw her in her room that night she said it looked like a young woman's face on an old woman's body or a body that had been burnt somehow. It was hard for Hannah to pick details off the woman in the dark but she could see enough to know that there was something wrong with the body. Why does Emily seem to have an attraction to young females in the house like she did with the little girl before us? Also, is the woman Hannah had been seeing and that I talked to on the Ouija board even Emily at all? These are all hair raising questions that I lacked any definitive answers to.

Getting back to our conversation with Cara, when she talked about Emily she referred to her as "Em." She said that we should just look at her as a grandma who lives upstairs. Cara said that she used to see Emily five to six times a week and it was really no big deal. She said there was a rocking chair in her room that actually belonged to Emily when she was alive and Emily used to sit in it and rock while watching Cara play with her toys. She said the only time she ever knew Emily to be vicious was when her boyfriend was being violent with her and Emily flew out of the closet scaring the crap out of him. He was supposed to be staying in the house at the time but didn't return to sleep there for three days after the event. She talked about how loving Emily was and about how when Cara was pregnant Emily used to always wear a smile on her face when she saw her. She claimed that after she had her baby she would wake up in the middle of the night and Emily would be standing over her baby's crib. Emily would even go as far as to put the babies blanket back on or its pacifier back in its mouth when it fell out at night.

This whole conversation went well but left me with even more questions than when I started. Were we even dealing with Emily in our house or was it someone else? Following the recommendations of family members, we contacted a Ghost Hunter's Society and set up a time for them to come to the house. The particular group we contacted had a psychic, Jeff, whom they used to clear the ghosts from the home. They said he was a very religious man who "brought peace wherever he went" and was particularly good at helping lost spirits move on. They said he had a one hundred percent house clearing success rate and if he didn't get them out the first time he would come back to the house until he did.

We were fortunate enough to talk to the psychic on the phone before he came down to get a remote reading and to help him to get a feel for what he was getting himself into. We gave him permission to do a reading of our house and all the individual family members in it by phone. When he did this he was overwhelmed saying "there is a LOT of stuff going on in your house." He said he saw five spirits in our home and a cat. He saw a woman upstairs (possibly Emily?), a woman in our garage, someone in our kitchen, a younger girl in our attic, and a man in the house named Albert. He said all the spirits in the house were being controlled by some stronger negative spirit and Albert in particular was having a lot of anxiety about this situation and he wanted help as did all the spirits in the home. Who Albert was, at the time, we had no clue. And to hear that there were five spirits in the house was shocking. He went on to tell us that there was a portal in our basement but didn't elaborate on this much. We were wondering if this portal was a possible explanation for the strange time warps that occasionally occurred here. He told us of a girl who was in our attic. He said that she was a mischievous spirit who used to get locked in our attic for misbehaving. She was up there still and has been for quite some time. He also said she likes to influence Hannah to "do bad things." He warned us never to lock Hannah in the attic, like we ever would, and never to let her be up there alone. I get chills wondering why he would warn us against that, thinking about what would happen if we did.

Then he started to read us individually looking for anything out of the ordinary. When he got to me he said that I had at first what looked like two but was actually three "attachments" on me that were using up my life energy. This would explain the drastic mood swings, and near nervous breakdown I almost had at work a few days before. I've never had anything like that in my life but one day I just thought I was going to lose my mind. I was glad to hear that there actually may have been an outside cause for my trouble and not necessarily something wrong with me. He claimed the "critters" were left over from my Ouija board experience and had latched on to me because they were curious about life and wanted to experience it through me. This being enough for us at the time we cut the phone conversation short and set up a time for him to come to the house. When my Dad got off the phone he kept thinking about Albert. Then suddenly remembering where he had seen the name he got out the abstract of the home to do a quick owner check on its history. Sure enough when we looked at the recent history of the home Betty Davis's husband who had died in the house was named Russell "Albert" Davis.

After talking to the psychic on the phone we felt confident about having him come with the ghost hunters to the house. The week before they were to come to the house I received three warnings from friends back at school including the bishop at my church in Murray against having the psychic come to the house. But I still felt it was what needed to be done and that this was God's way of sending help to us, using the psychic as a vessel to do his work. I was still uncertain about what should be done and prayed the night before the ghost hunters came that if God didn't want them to come he should stop them somehow.

The day they were to come I got off work early and came home. When I got home my whole family was upset to read an email the ghost hunters had sent earlier that day proclaiming that they had been vandalized and wouldn't be able to make it. For some reason this wasn't good enough for me and despite my prayer I still at least wanted Jeff to come. We talked to Jeff on the phone and he said he was still willing to come the following weekend if we would have him. After some debate we decided it was the thing to do, for I wanted to get this taken care of and we were running out of time before I went back to school. Anxiously awaiting the arrival of the psychic we prepared ourselves for the experience and were really looking forward to it.

Chapter Eleven

Into the light...

The day of the psychic's visit arrived and my Dad, Mom, brother and I were all waiting patiently in the living room for him when he showed up. He was a shorter man with a thick mustache and a slightly crooked walk. He was very cheerful and greeted us with a warm smile and a handshake. When he came in the house he didn't even want to walk around and see the rooms. He just sat in the living room the whole time and was able to communicate with everyone from there. We talked a little about the spirits and he told us about his drive down from Chicago and what he had talked about with them. He said the woman in our garage was going to be the hardest to get to cross over. He said she had been raped and left for dead on the land where our garage was now built. All her life her parents had drilled into her head that if she had sex out of wedlock she would be thrown in hell. So when she died, even though she was raped, she was too scared to go into the light. He explained that these spirits that were in limbo, sharing basically the same world with us that is only separated by a thin line, really don't know anymore about God, Jesus, or what happens when you enter the light than we do. That's why it's so important for them to find someone that can communicate with them and knows about these things.

Jeff then talked more about the young fourteen year old girl in our attic. He said she had been restrained up there for five to six years at one point. We don't know how she died but she had been up in that attic ever since and really hated it up there. He said she was very eager to leave but didn't want to leave her cat and her dog behind. I was wondering when he said this if the girl he was referring to was in fact the one whom my sister saw in her room that night and that was her cat that was with her.

Throughout the conversation Jeff would often be looking around to the corners of the room as the spirits moved about. It was as though he was just watching them and we couldn't see a thing. When he first walked in the house our dog Conner started getting overly excited and jumping on Jeff to get his attention. After this happened a few times Jeff started snapping his fingers and looking Conner in the eye. After a few snaps Conner completely calmed down and laid in the middle of the room for the rest of the time Jeff was there.

I really wanted to know about my Ouija board experience and if I had ever talked to anyone from the house at all. This turned the attention towards me. He said that I had in fact talked with spirits from the house on the board. He said that the spirits in the home knew that when we moved in I would be the one to set the process in motion for their chance to move on.

At my request he started to look at my past lives. Some of the things I had done in my past lives were startling but the biggest thing he told me was that I had once walked with Jesus Christ when he was here with us on earth. He said I was an interpreter for the words of Jesus into a tongue that he couldn't even pronounce. Jeff told me that the reason I feel anxiety a lot is because of what I had done in my most recent life. Apparently I was a victim of starvation in the holocaust, often skipping my few and far between meals so others, primarily children, could eat. He said I had a part in building the pyramids, and was even around when Napoleon was alive and fighting wars in France. He confirmed that I was Stonewall Jackson in a past life and that my Dad and I had in fact done many things together in past lives. Jeff went on to tell me I had once caused a lot of trouble robbing banks and trains and was eventually hanged for my mischief. He said that I was currently a part of the "indigo generation," born with a higher conscience and spiritual awareness. He said this was the cause for all the weird stuff happening to me on the Ouija board.

After we sat in the living room and talked with Jeff for hours he finally got on with the spirit clearing. He went down in the basement in the dark asking us not to turn on any lights. After he disappeared he came back up about fifteen to twenty minutes later. He said that everything had gone really well and, oddly enough, on his way back up the stairs a very small boy ran out from beneath the stairs and latched onto his leg. He informed us that he was going to take the boy home and care for him there, eventually helping the young, scared spirit to move on. After this he asked me to go outside with him so he could remove the attachments from my lower back. Here he was talking about the "critters" that had attached themselves to me when I was involved with the Ouija board. I was anxious to have them off but was unsure of what to expect when he removed them from me. I went out there with him and he placed his hands on my back asking me to relax. It took me a while to get comfortable but after a few minutes he started moving his hands across my back. Eventually he informed me that he was finished and we immediately ran in the house trying to escape the mosquitoes. I felt the same as I had before we went outside but I didn't expect to feel any lighter or anything when it was all done. We thanked Jeff and told him goodbye. He left just as peacefully as he came, telling us to call or write him with questions anytime.

That night I went out and had a great time with my friends. I actually did feel better than normal and just couldn't stop smiling. As I write this it has been a few days since Jeff left and I can honestly say that I feel as though the house has become much quieter. I am not sensing anything when I go upstairs and have started sleeping up there again. My energy level during the day has increased considerably and I feel like I finally have some closure to this whole experience that seemed to drag on forever. It has been a wild ride, at times it seemed like it would never end, but I have learned so much in this spiritual awakening of sorts on so many levels that I can say I am grateful for having been allowed to bare witness to the whole thing. I always knew that I would never be a person to believe in God on blind faith. I could never just surrender to text as being truth without actually having any experiences on my own as proof of an afterlife. I believe he put me through all of this, knowing that my faith would come out ten times stronger in the end. I hope my story alone will at least inspire some thought in those that pick it up. I know it has been cause for a lot of freaked out friends on long nights of discussing what caused the "new Abe" to come back after his first semester at school. It has been a long run to this point for my family but I wouldn't trade in a moment of it for anything. The experience has become an important thread in the binding of this family and we won't soon forget what we've been through together in our house on Kansas Street.

Chapter Twelve

A year of reflection...

It has been almost a year since my sister saw Emily in her room that night and since Jeff came to cleanse our home. I have had a lot of time to think about all the things that have happened and at times my curiosity for the subject and all there is to think about can be overwhelming to me. I have spent the last year as an RA in Elizabeth and my story is one that has been circulated amongst a pretty large group of people in the dorm. Nothing has happened to us in our home in the past year, it has been rather quiet and normal. I think back to the times when the story was at its height and I am still amazed at how incredible the entire experience was. It's so weird to have been in the thick of experiencing other levels of existence and then have to return to a life where supernatural things are just stories and infrequent topics of conversation. There are often times when I want to go back to those days and ask more questions and examine situations even more closely than before. I want to learn more about the afterlife, ghosts, and God but I feel that if I were to try and satisfy such suspicion that I would be violating some rules or possibly getting myself into something that I may not be able to get out of this time. I have made new friends, some of whom are very much like I used to be, thinking that little exists beyond our own sight and circumstances. I want to be able to take them and show them the things that I have experienced but that would require me to reacquire habits that I have sworn off like talking on the Ouija board. Sometimes I think it would almost be worth the personal consequences to open another's eyes to what I have seen and to the world that exists both with and beyond our own.

I have had three noteworthy experiences since I went back to school that I am going to include in this chapter. The first has more to do with my own faith journey than anything but I am going to include it to give an example of how frustration and confusion seem to have grown out of this entire experience as much as if not more than clarity and revelation.

At the beginning of this year I was coming out of a life changing summer that not only included a visitation from Emily and a ghost clearing psychic but where I had also read some excellent books concerning the spiritual questions I had swimming around in my head. My reading over the summer had shown me the value that exists in many of the world's religions. I saw how God is much greater and mysterious than he exists within the confines of certain doctrines and that is why it is better to seek after him directly than through a protocol of exoteric tradition or one correct way as so many religions teach. Since I had been back to school I had been battling with people telling me that I had "strayed from the path." They were basically just trying to get me to doubt any of these new ideas I had and just get back to using the Bible as my one and only source. This was troubling me a great deal and, not knowing where to turn, I made a deal with God. It was early in the semester and I had gone to a church called the Abundant Life Christian Center with some friends one Sunday morning. As I was standing in church that day I told God that if he gave the bishop a message for me in that moment I would accept the Bible for what it is and not question it anymore. Seconds later, the bishop looked up from whatever he was doing and pointed to me in the crowd and told me to come stand up front with him. He gave me this long talk about my destiny and how it was so important that I got right with God, and soon! I was so confused when this was happening but at the same time happy because I felt like I had received the message from God I was looking for. In time this incident would serve to be simply not good enough. Possibilities of other explanations besides God giving me a direct message at my request began to enter my mind and once again I began to doubt the divinity involved in this experience. Even as I write this now I wonder how I can take such experiences and question them but there are too many unanswered questions in my mind for me to commit myself to a single religion. The topic of spirituality and matters of God are so incredibly important to me now and being so confused about them at times weighs on my mind very heavily.

Another incident I wanted to include in this chapter occurred as some of our neighbors began to hear about what went on in my house and the book I was writing. One day the youngest boy and I started talking about it after he had found one of my manuscripts in the basement and had been reading through some of it. He told me that they used to have a dog that died while they were living in their house. Shortly after the dogs death his older brother saw the dog running about in the back yard. He nervously continued to tell me that one night while he was trying to sleep in his room he opened his eyes and looked over to his doorway. There he said he saw a young girl dressed in green watching him. Out of fear he threw his blanket over his head and eventually fell asleep never going on to speak of the incident to anybody until now. These kinds of stories make me want to go door to door on my street and ask people if they've had any kind of paranormal experiences in their homes. Maybe there is something about the area where I live. Could the girl dressed in green that my neighbor saw in his room have been Emily? If not, I wonder if she had a part in this whole story or if her main role is still yet to come in the lives of others.

Another interesting thing that happened to me came just this last semester. I walked into a Sam Goody after dinner one night with my dorm shirt spelling Elizabeth College on the front in big letters. One of the employees came up to me and started talking about when he used to live in Elizabeth. He said he lived there almost six years ago and after talking to me for a while about all the crazy things he used to do there he made a comment about the "devil worship" that used to go on in Elizabeth before he walked out back to take out some trash. After he left I got to wondering if maybe he knew something that might connect with any of the experiences I had in Elizabeth. When he came back in the store I asked him if any of the "devil worship" he had heard of happened on the fifth floor. He said that the fifth floor is where he and his roommate used to live and that it was where they did everything they did that might be considered "devil worship." He told me he doesn't really consider it devil worship but that he uses that as a sort of buzz word to get people's attention. I got his name and number and met with him on campus one night to exchange stories. I found out that he and a bunch of other students, one of whom is now the president of the Student Pagan Association on campus, were involved in a lot of occult activity on the floor years ago. He said that they got their hands on some Indian symbol and decided it might be fun to go out to a local wooded park called Land Between the Lakes and construct the symbol out of sticks and stones to see what would happen. He said when they did this rocks started to fly around and one of his friends just walked to the edge of a short ledge overlooking the lake about eight feet down and just fell in the water. Terrified they grabbed their dazed friend out of the lake and jumped in their cars to drive back to the dorm. When they all got back to their room they were discussing what had happened and had the mutual feeling that something had followed them back.

He continued to deal with the occult, using the Ouija board among other things. His experiences started out as the sound of coins dropping on the floor above him all night long. He complained to his RA and when they went to check on the room above them they found that the residents had been out of town for the past few days. One night he was on the Ouija board and he saw a girl up in the corner of his room. He said he kept seeing this girl who appeared to him and at one point she even appeared for a split second in place of his reflection in the mirror of his dorm room. He said that if the university offered to erase his thousands and thousands of dollars worth of debt and enhance his graduating G.P.A to a 3.0 if he would just spend another night in room 513, he wouldn't do it due to the things he and his friends saw there. I found this very interesting because it showed me that there was actually stuff going on in Elizabeth College that dealt with the occult long before I even got there. There is something that seems to dwell on the fifth floor of that dorm and I don't know what it was those kids brought back with them that night but whatever it was seems to still be there to this day.

At this point I still hunger for a greater awareness about how the world works, and about all the various levels to our world that exist beyond our immediate perceptions. Sometimes I wonder where Emily and JT are right now. Emily isn't in my house anymore, is she in heaven, has she found her family, her friends, a new life? I would really like to have an expanded understanding of the events that went on in this house because there are still many things that happened that we really don't have good explanations for. What was it about this house that caused all these ghosts to stick around anyway? Someday we may even knock down that wall in the cellar and see whatever it is that lies behind it, or maybe we'll do that right before we move out. I hope to have the answers to these questions someday but have currently settled to put them asleep in my mind because otherwise they would drive me crazy. As for now, I have this small timeless book that will forever serve as a chronicle of what has happened in this incredible house. Hopefully it will find its way into the hands of an audience that will be as moved by the story as my family has been. On the day we move out I fully plan to make my last action a trip upstairs and into that closet in the room where I grew up. There I will leave a single copy of this book in that small place to lie in solitude and collect dust until its inevitable discovery by a new family. I can only hope that when it is found the book will contain only a story from the past and not an affirmation to the odd experiences of its finder. As for me the book is the final chapter of a long journey that ventured well beyond menacing old shutters or a bump in the night.

In the end I can look back and see that this has been an incredible personal journey for myself, as through it all I have found a new sense of life, spirituality, God, and a woman upstairs named Emily.

Printed in the United States
59280LVS00001B/103-105